31143011332518
J 304.2022 Richards, J
Richards, Jon, 1970-
author, illustrator.
People on Earth : who we
are and how we live in
maps and infographics

J

DISCARD

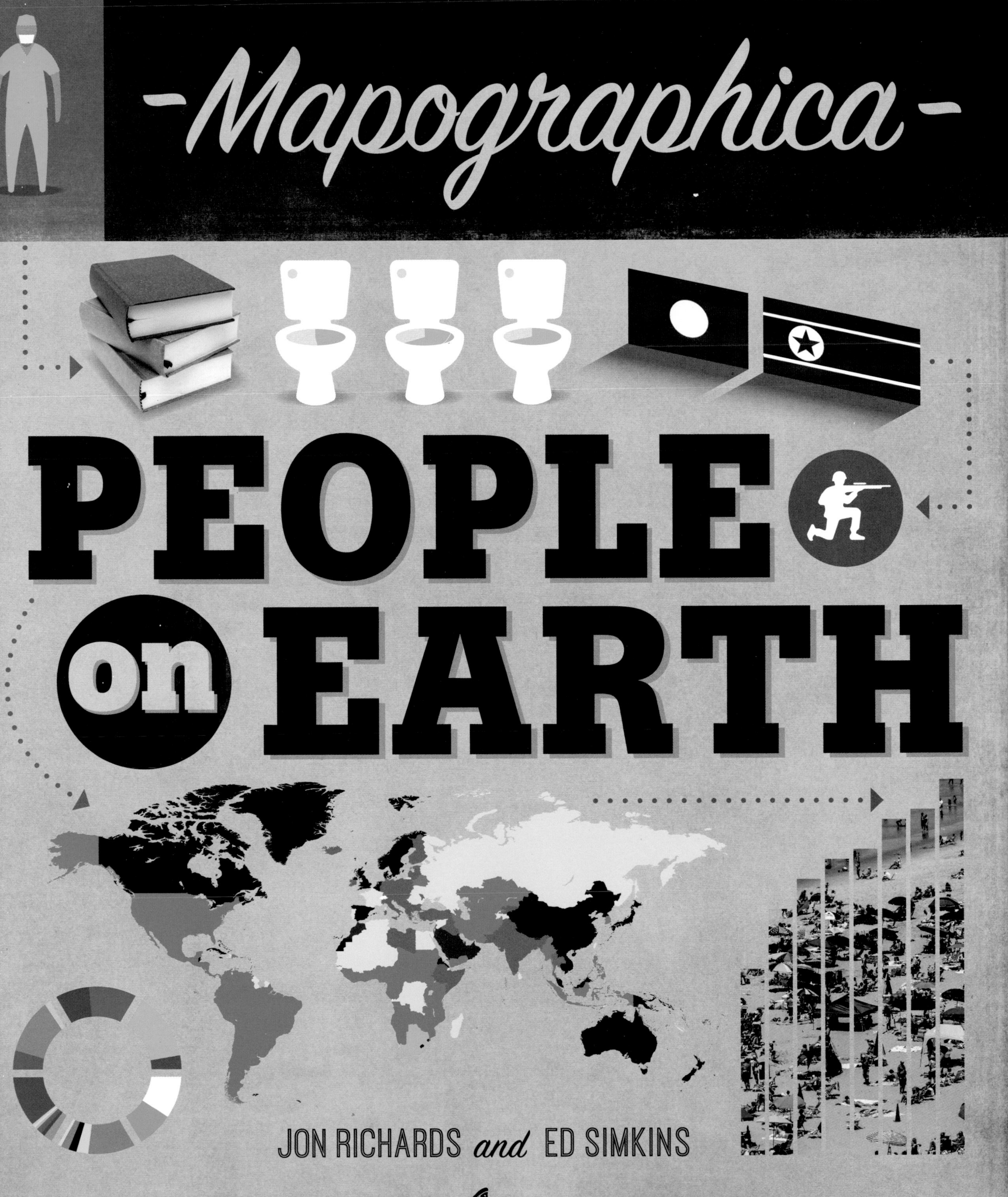

Mapographica

PEOPLE on EARTH

JON RICHARDS *and* ED SIMKINS

WAYLAND

CONTENTS

ACKNOWLEDGEMENTS

First published in Great Britain in 2015
by Wayland
Copyright © Wayland, 2015
All rights reserved
Editor: Julia Adams
Produced for Wayland by Tall Tree Ltd
Designer: Ed Simkins
Editor: Jon Richards

Dewey number: 304.2'0223-dc23
ISBN 978 0 7502 9151 4

Wayland, an imprint of
Hachette Children's Group
Part of Hodder and Stoughton
Carmelite House
50 Victoria Embankment
London EC4Y 0DZ

An Hachette UK Company
www.hachette.co.uk
www.hachettechildrens.co.uk

Printed and bound in Malaysia

10 9 8 7 6 5 4 3 2 1

Picture credits can be found on page 32

The world in 100 PEOPLE

If you reduced the world's population to just 100 people, then an 'average' person would live in a town in Asia, speak Chinese, be able to read and write, be between 15 and 64 years old, and would not be undernourished or overweight.

OVERWEIGHT (ADULTS OVER 18)

Overweight and obese **39** *Undernourished* **11** *Underweight or OK* **50**

AGE

26 *0–14 years old*
66 *15–64 years old*
8 *65 and older*

LITERACY

Can read and write **83**
Can't read and write **17**

URBANISATION

Live in towns **54**
Live in the country **46**

FIRST LANGUAGE

Chinese **12**
Spanish **5**
English **5**
Arabic **3**
Hindi **3**
Bengali **3**
Portuguese **3**
Other **66**

POPULATION DISTRIBUTION

Asia **60** *Europe* **11** *North America* **5**
Africa **15** *Latin America and Caribbean* **9**

The world is divided into large landmasses, called continents. The 7 billion people who live on the planet are not scattered evenly across these continents – more than 60 per cent of these people live in just one continent, Asia.

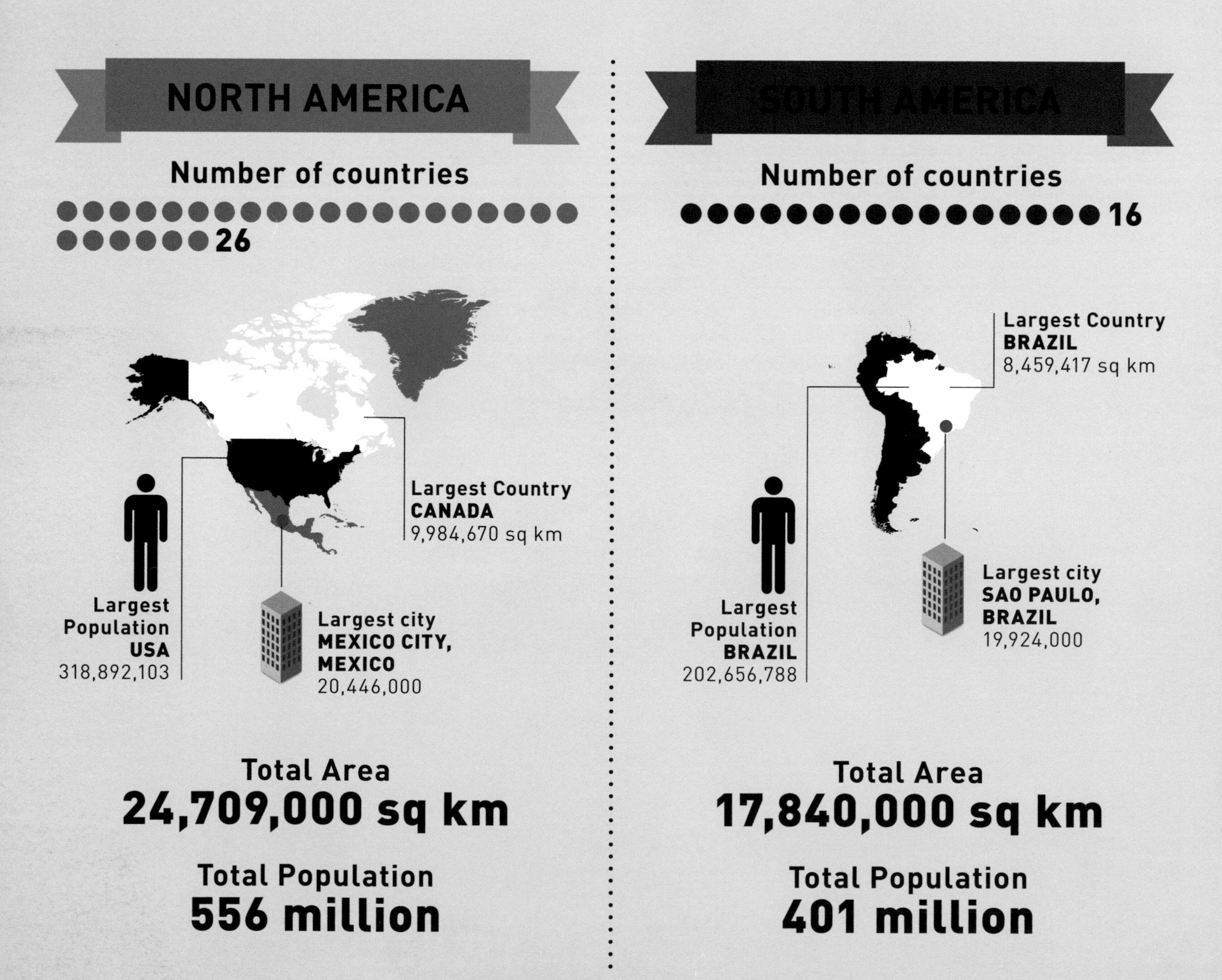

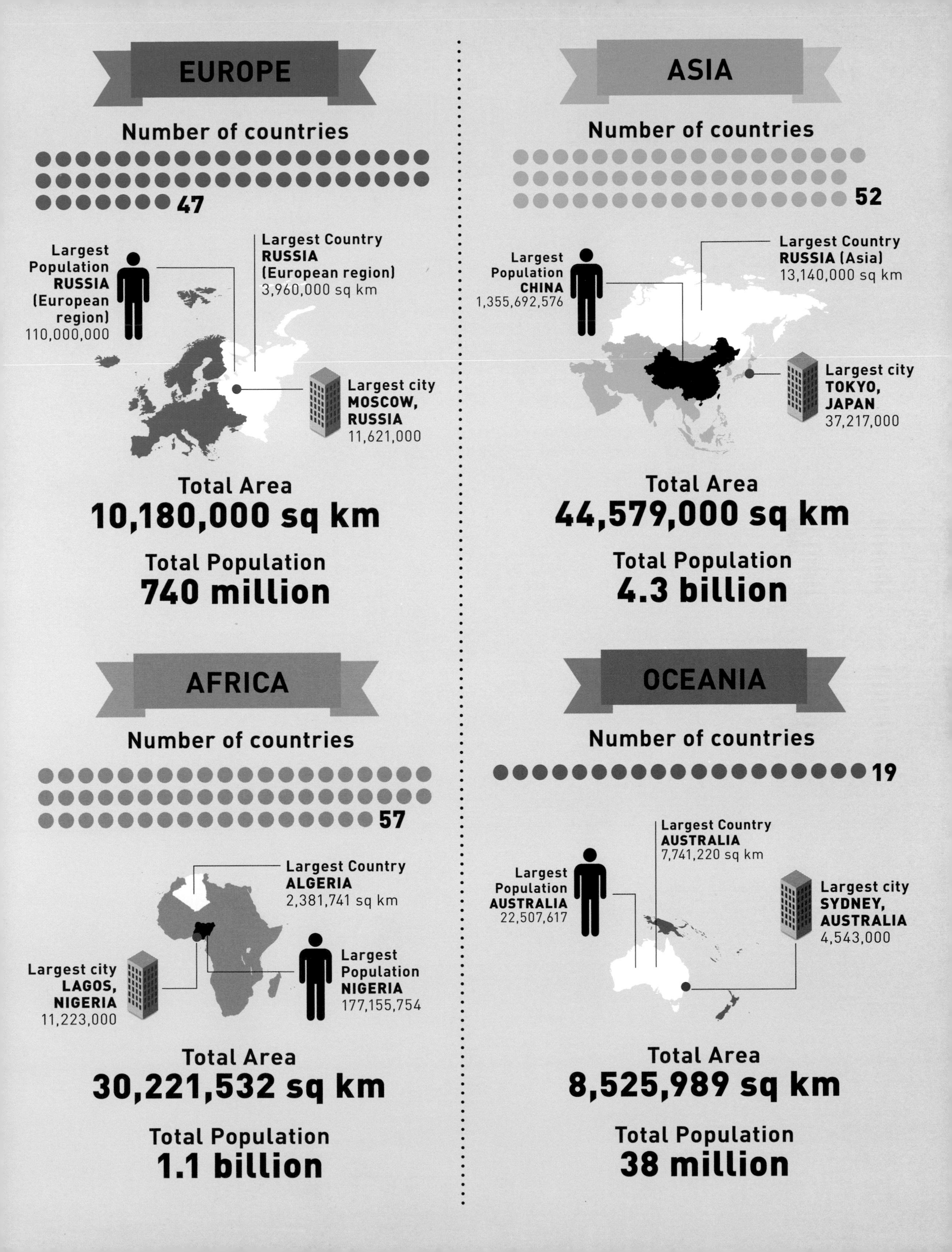
EUROPE
Number of countries
47
Largest Population
RUSSIA
(European region)
110,000,000
Largest Country
RUSSIA
(European region)
3,960,000 sq km
Largest city
MOSCOW, RUSSIA
11,621,000
Total Area
10,180,000 sq km
Total Population
740 million
ASIA
Number of countries
52
Largest Population
CHINA
1,355,692,576
Largest Country
RUSSIA (Asia)
13,140,000 sq km
Largest city
TOKYO, JAPAN
37,217,000
Total Area
44,579,000 sq km
Total Population
4.3 billion
AFRICA
Number of countries
57
Largest Country
ALGERIA
2,381,741 sq km
Largest city
LAGOS, NIGERIA
11,223,000
Largest Population
NIGERIA
177,155,754
Total Area
30,221,532 sq km
Total Population
1.1 billion
OCEANIA
Number of countries
19
Largest Country
AUSTRALIA
7,741,220 sq km
Largest Population
AUSTRALIA
22,507,617
Largest city
SYDNEY, AUSTRALIA
4,543,000
Total Area
8,525,989 sq km
Total Population
38 million

Human ORIGINS

Modern humans, *Homo sapiens*, first appeared in Africa about 200,000 years ago. However, it was another 130,000–140,000 years before they started to move out of Africa. By about 50,000 years ago, they had reached Southeast Asia and Australia.

MIGRATION OF MODERN HUMANS

Driven by the need for food and a place to settle, humans started to migrate out of Africa to other parts of the world.

'Cradle of humanity'
This region around the East African Rift Valley is where the earliest human remains have been found. From this point, modern humans set out to colonise the planet.

40k

25k

60k

50k

160k

195k

65k

155k

Into Australia
During the ice age, about 50,000 years ago, large amounts of water were frozen as ice sheets. Sea levels dropped so much that a land bridge formed, allowing humans to walk from Southeast Asia to Australia.

KEY

195k **Human finds** (195,000,000 years old)

65k **Human migration** (65,000 years ago)

Route of migration

Other possible routes

TIMELINE

Emergence of modern humans in Africa

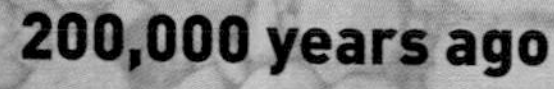

200,000 years ago

80,000 years ago

Ice age begins

Population explosion in Africa

78,000 years ago

Modern humans begin to leave Africa

65,000 years ago

Modern humans spread across S.E. Asia

FAMILY TREE

The earliest human ancestors appeared more than 6 million years ago (MYA). Several different groups evolved, before our direct ancestors, the *Homo* group, appeared about 2 million years ago.

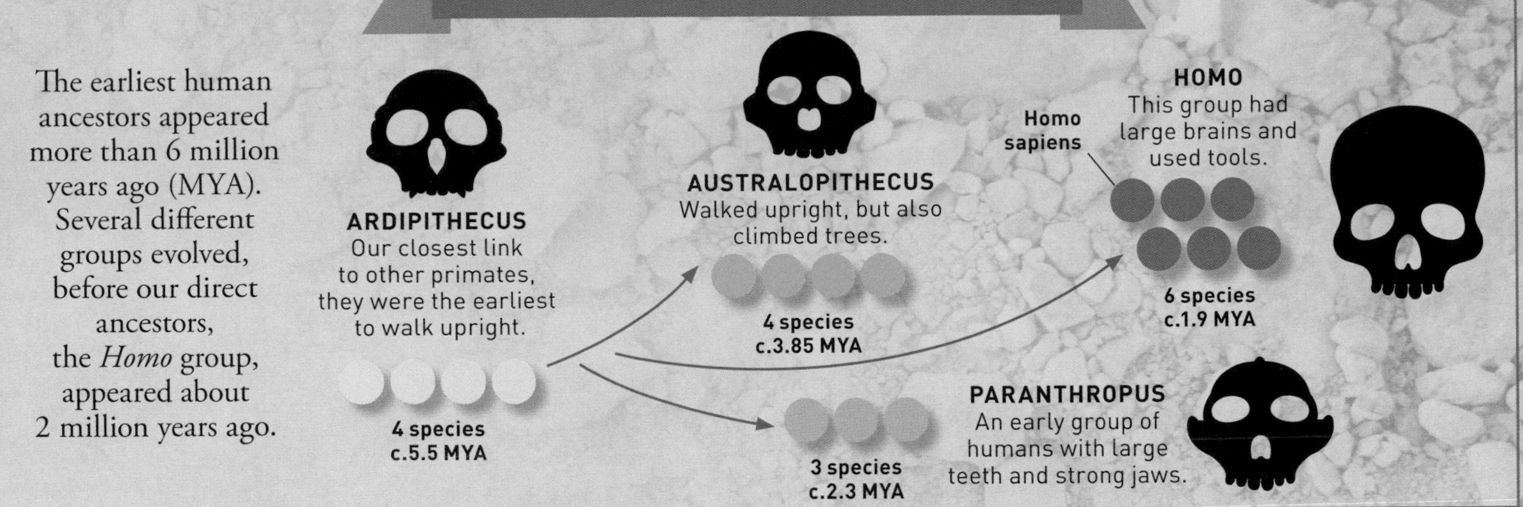

16k

Land bridge
About 16,000 years ago, a land bridge formed linking Siberia to America. Humans crossed this land bridge. They were following herds of animals that used the bridge as a migration route.

16k

Hawaii

Micronesia

Melanesia

Easter Island

50k

15k

Crossing the Pacific

Having settled in Southeast Asia and Australia, humans faced the enormous Pacific Ocean. Despite it measuring more than 5,000 km across, human settlers undertook epic voyages starting about 4,000 years ago with expansion into Micronesia and Melanesia, and finishing with the settlement of Hawaii and Easter Island at the start of the 14th century.

Modern humans reach Australia
50,000 years ago

Modern humans populate Europe
35,000 years ago

Modern humans populate Americas
20,000 years ago

Ice age ends
8,000 years ago

Today

— Population — GROWTH

How quickly a country grows depends on a number of things, including the standard of healthcare, how many children are born, how long people live for and how rich they are. While the populations of some countries and regions are growing very quickly, others are predicted to get smaller!

MOST POPULATED COUNTRIES

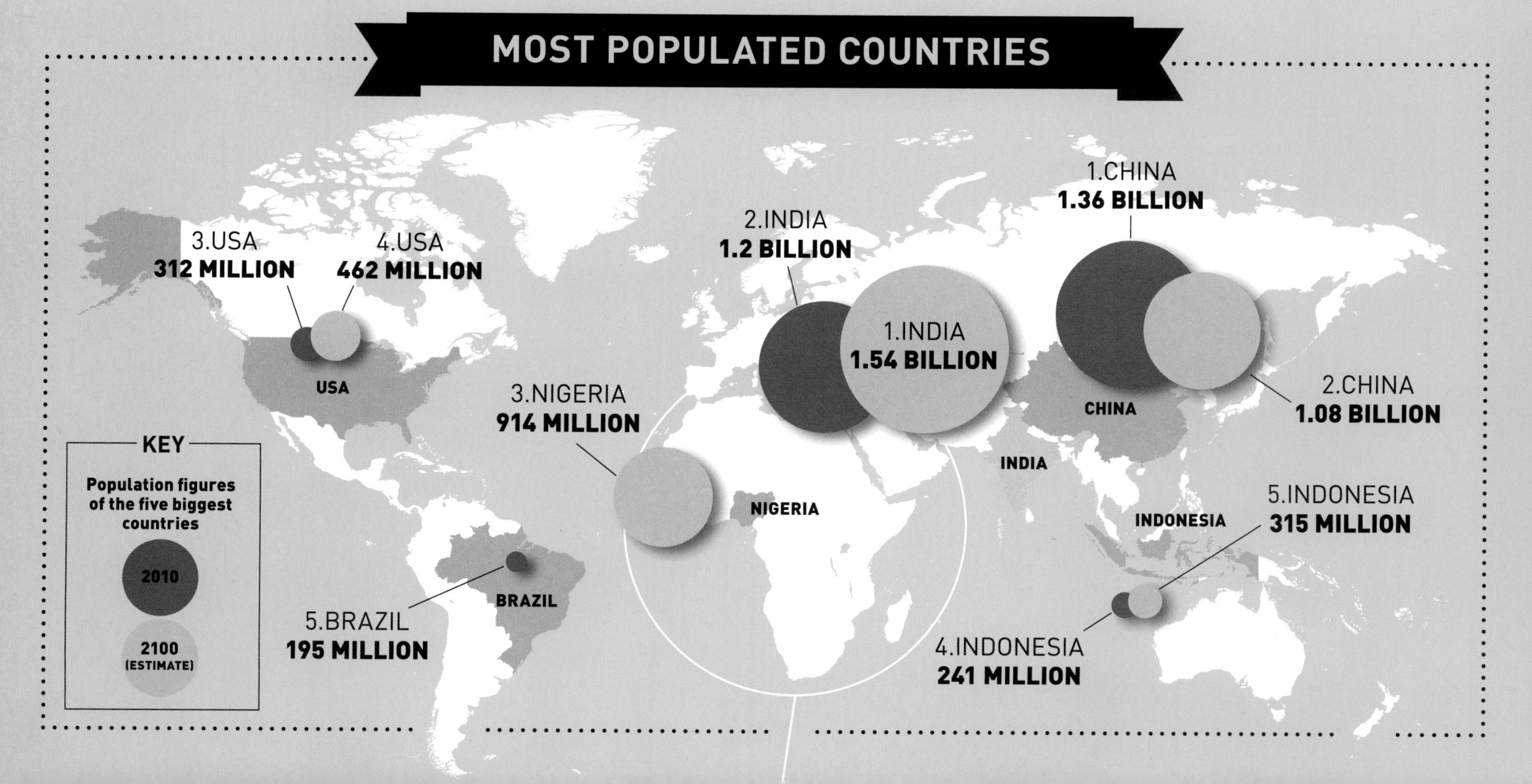

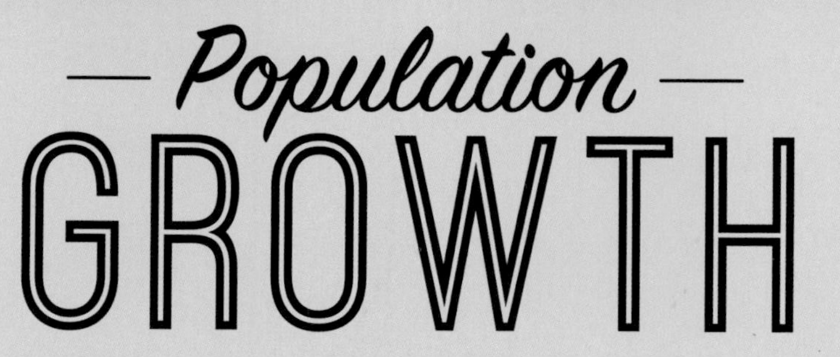

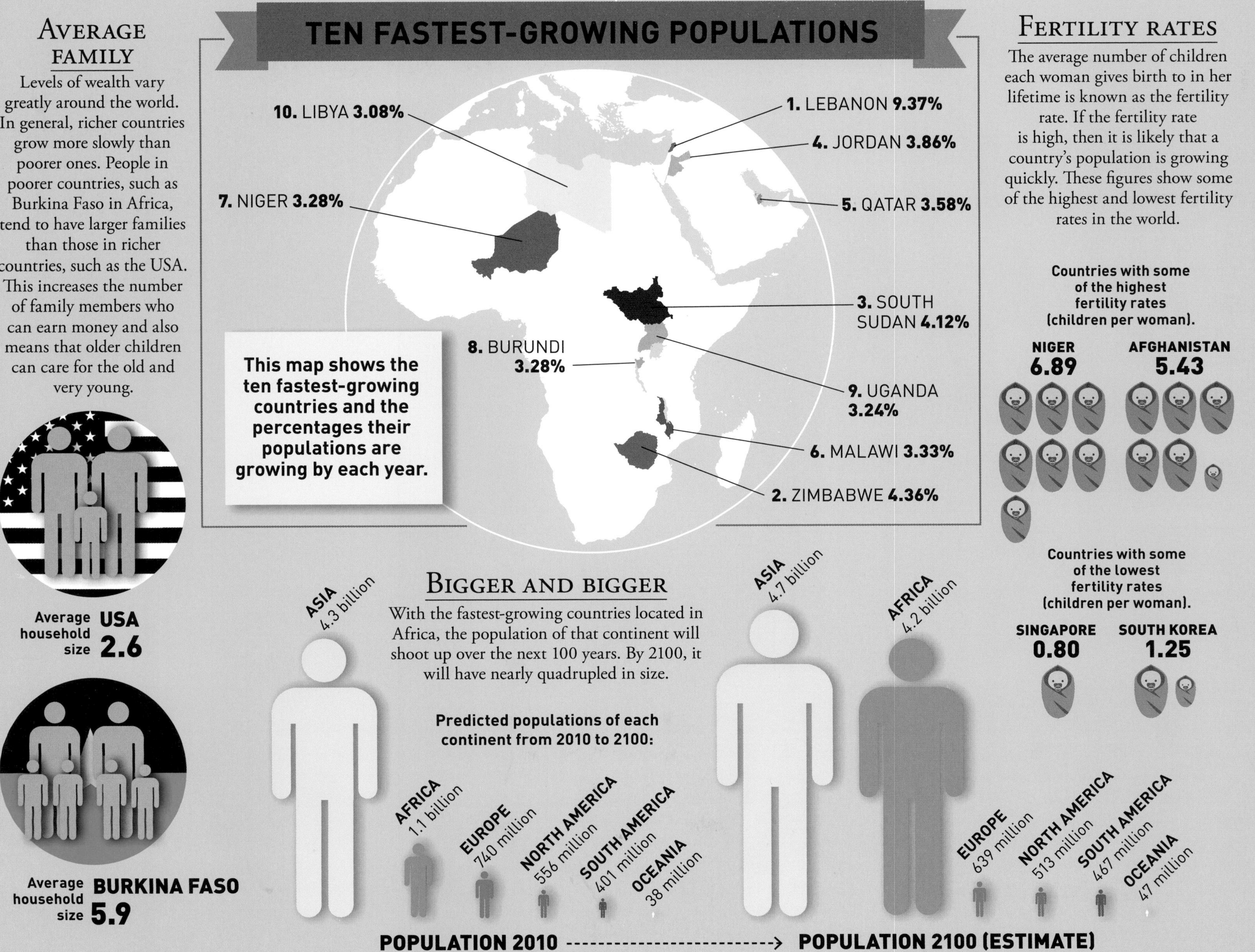

AVERAGE FAMILY
Levels of wealth vary greatly around the world. In general, richer countries grow more slowly than poorer ones. People in poorer countries, such as Burkina Faso in Africa, tend to have larger families than those in richer countries, such as the USA. This increases the number of family members who can earn money and also means that older children can care for the old and very young.
Average household size USA 2.6
Average household size BURKINA FASO 5.9
TEN FASTEST-GROWING POPULATIONS
10. LIBYA 3.08%
7. NIGER 3.28%
1. LEBANON 9.37%
4. JORDAN 3.86%
5. QATAR 3.58%
3. SOUTH SUDAN 4.12%
8. BURUNDI 3.28%
9. UGANDA 3.24%
6. MALAWI 3.33%
2. ZIMBABWE 4.36%
This map shows the ten fastest-growing countries and the percentages their populations are growing by each year.
FERTILITY RATES
The average number of children each woman gives birth to in her lifetime is known as the fertility rate. If the fertility rate is high, then it is likely that a country's population is growing quickly. These figures show some of the highest and lowest fertility rates in the world.
Countries with some of the highest fertility rates (children per woman).
NIGER 6.89
AFGHANISTAN 5.43
Countries with some of the lowest fertility rates (children per woman).
SINGAPORE 0.80
SOUTH KOREA 1.25
BIGGER AND BIGGER
With the fastest-growing countries located in Africa, the population of that continent will shoot up over the next 100 years. By 2100, it will have nearly quadrupled in size.
Predicted populations of each continent from 2010 to 2100:
ASIA 4.3 billion
AFRICA 1.1 billion
EUROPE 740 million
NORTH AMERICA 556 million
SOUTH AMERICA 401 million
OCEANIA 38 million
ASIA 4.7 billion
AFRICA 4.2 billion
EUROPE 639 million
NORTH AMERICA 513 million
SOUTH AMERICA 467 million
OCEANIA 47 million
POPULATION 2010 ------------------------> POPULATION 2100 (ESTIMATE)

A LONG LIFE?

Today, the average life expectancy around the world is 70, with men living an average of 68 years and women 73 years. How long you live depends on how wealthy you are, whether or not you have access to sanitation (including a toilet!) and the quality of your diet.

AVERAGE AGES

The richer a country is, and the more its population earns – measured in Gross Domestic Product (GDP) per person – the longer its population usually lives.

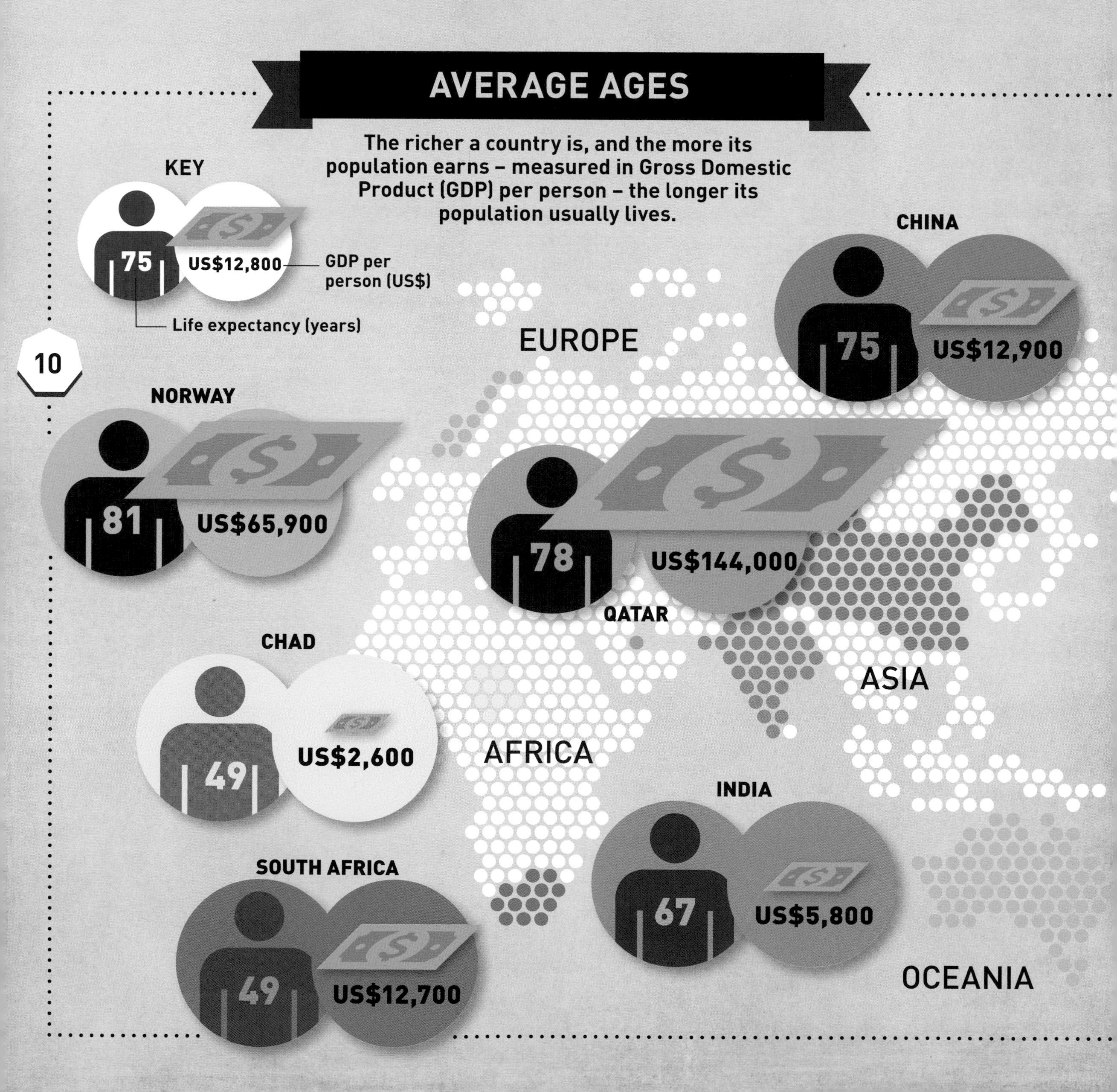

KEEP IT CLEAN

Countries with good sanitation are able to get rid of human waste cleanly and effectively. This can prevent the spread of fatal diseases and increases the life expectancy, allowing people to live longer, healthier lives.

Every 20 seconds
a child dies as a result of poor sanitation.

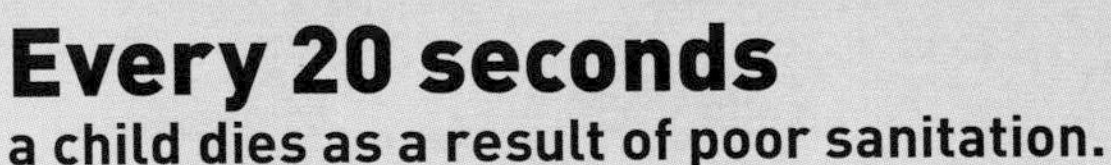

1990 **49%** 2010 **63%** 2015 **67%**

Access to sanitation (% of world population)

Access to sanitation (% of country's population)

SOUTH SUDAN **16%** KENYA **31%**

INDONESIA **71%** PANAMA **80%** GERMANY **100%**

The World Bank lists 38 countries whose people have 100% access to improved sanitation facilities. These include the USA, the UK, Greenland, Saudi Arabia, Australia and South Korea.

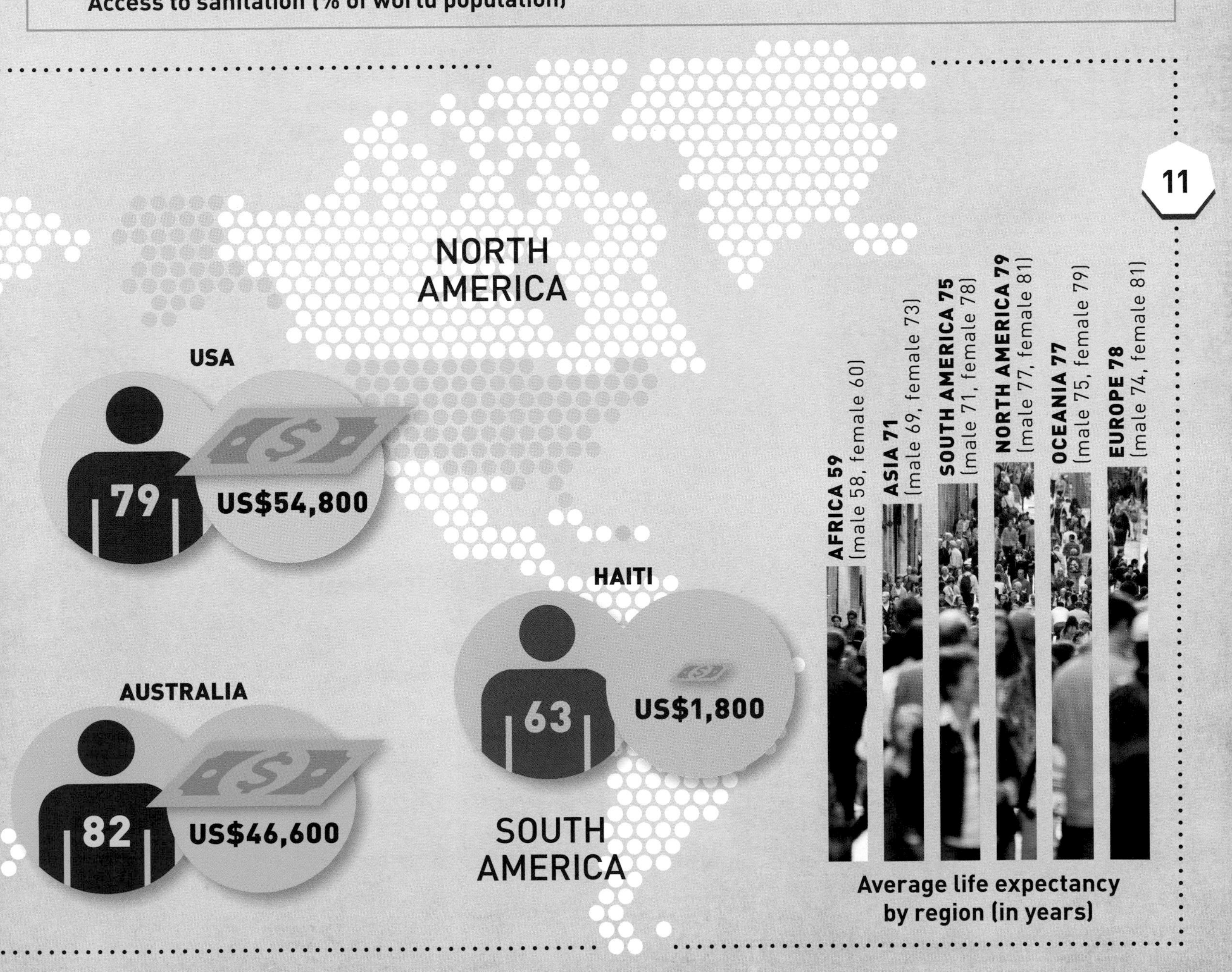

Average life expectancy by region (in years)

Diseases and DOCTORS

Death from disease is a constant threat in any part of the world. Key to fighting disease is a country's health service and the number of doctors and facilities available.

MOST LIKELY CAUSES OF DEATH

This world map shows the diseases and conditions that cause the greatest number of deaths in each country.

Lithuania

San Marino

Spain

CAUSE OF DEATH

- HEART DISEASE
- CANCER
- HIV/AIDS
- TUBERCULOSIS
- KIDNEY DISEASE
- LIVER DISEASE
- RESPIRATORY INFECTION
- No data available

DISEASE AND WEALTH

The wealth of a country can decide the diseases its people are most susceptible to. People living in poorer countries are more likely to die from infectious diseases, because their countries have fewer doctors and health facilities. People in richer countries are more likely to die from conditions caused by bad habits, such as smoking.

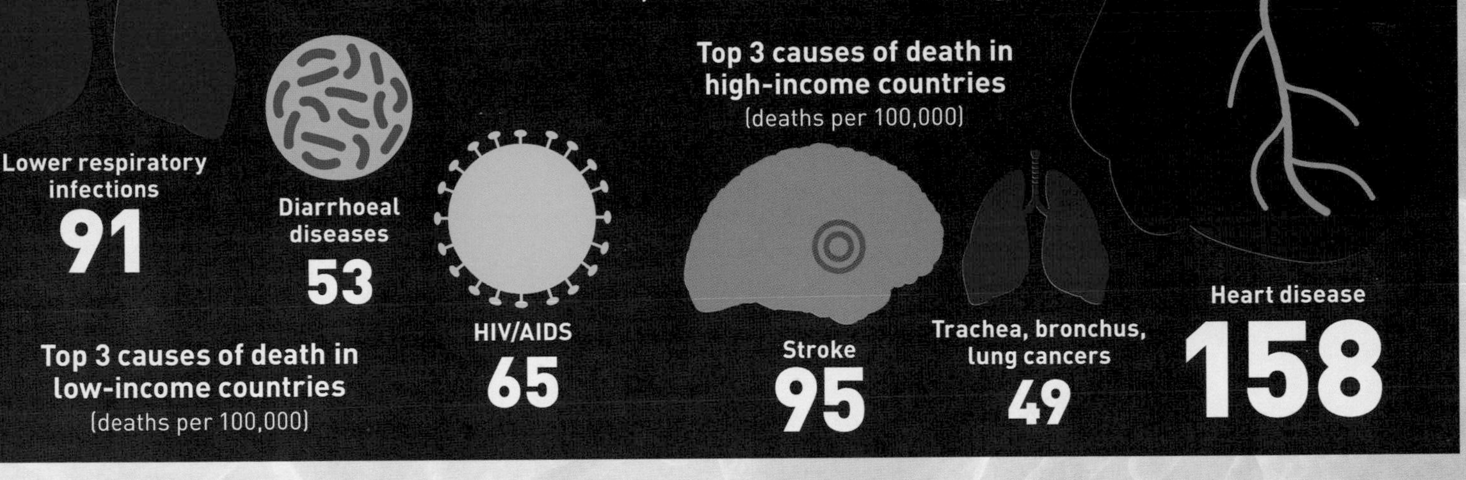

Georgia
Bhutan
Laos
Qatar
Cambodia
Indonesia
Mozambique

Doctors

Countries with a high number of doctors are likely to have a good standard of healthcare, helping to prevent and control diseases. According to the World Health Organisation, fewer than 2.3 health workers (doctors, nurses and midwives) per 1,000 people is not enough to meet healthcare needs. These figures show how many doctors there are for every 1,000 people.

LOWEST

Mozambique 0.1
Laos 0.2
Indonesia 0.2
Cambodia 0.2
Bhutan 0.3

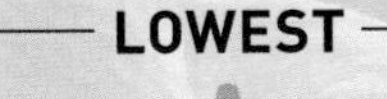

HIGHEST

Qatar 7.7 doctors per 1,000 people
San Marino 5.1
Georgia 4.2
Lithuania 4.1
Spain 3.7

— *Living in* —
CITIES

Since the earliest cities were founded more than 10,000 years ago, more and more people have been moving to live in urban settlements. This movement of people from the country to cities is called urbanisation.

PEOPLE LIVING IN URBAN AREAS
AND CITIES WITH MORE THAN 10 MILLION PEOPLE

This map shows the percentage of people that live in towns and cities in each country around the world.

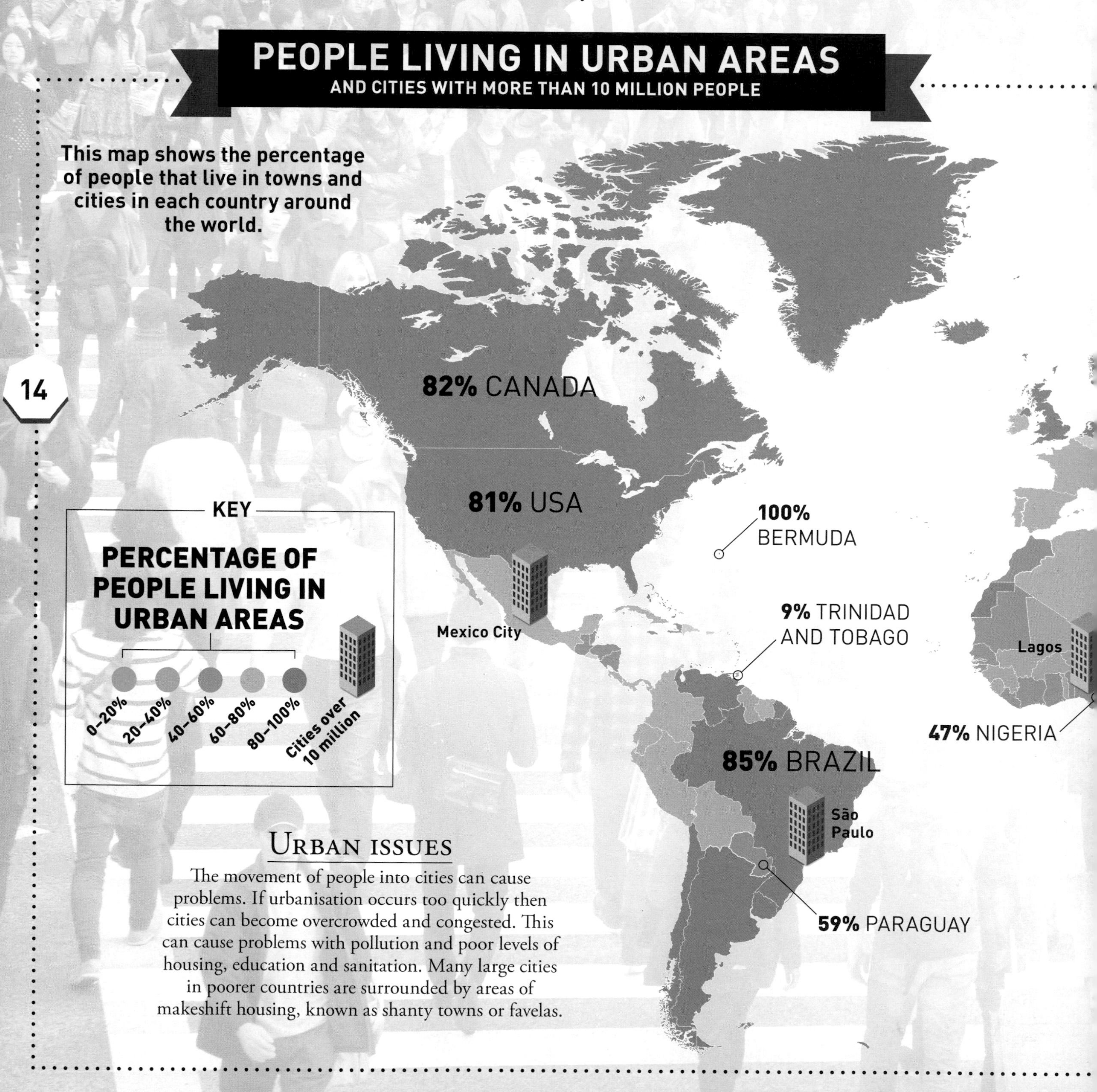

URBAN ISSUES

The movement of people into cities can cause problems. If urbanisation occurs too quickly then cities can become overcrowded and congested. This can cause problems with pollution and poor levels of housing, education and sanitation. Many large cities in poorer countries are surrounded by areas of makeshift housing, known as shanty towns or favelas.

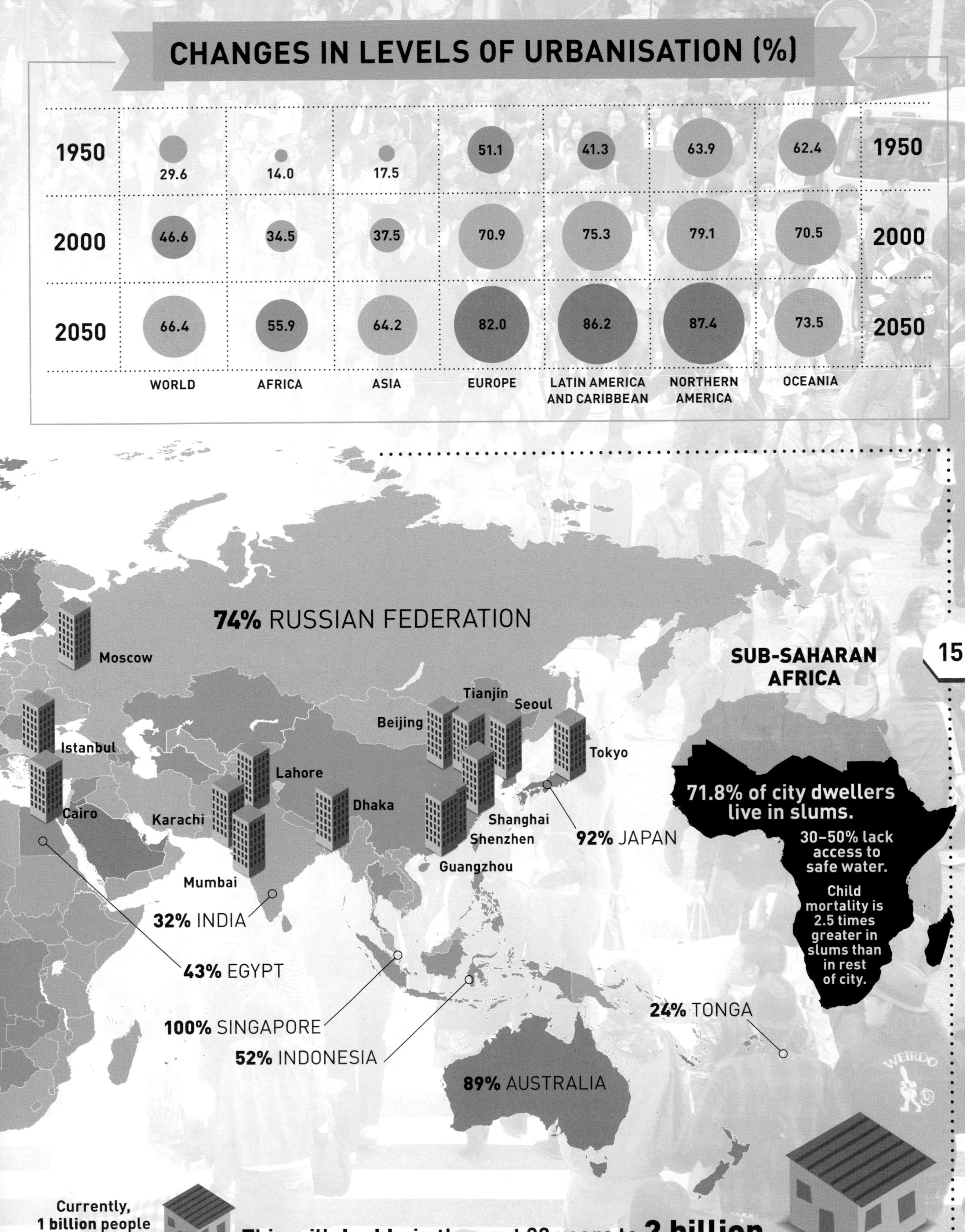
CHANGES IN LEVELS OF URBANISATION (%)
1950
29.6
14.0
17.5
51.1
41.3
63.9
62.4
1950
2000
46.6
34.5
37.5
70.9
75.3
79.1
70.5
2000
2050
66.4
55.9
64.2
82.0
86.2
87.4
73.5
2050
WORLD
AFRICA
ASIA
EUROPE
LATIN AMERICA AND CARIBBEAN
NORTHERN AMERICA
OCEANIA
74% RUSSIAN FEDERATION
Moscow
Istanbul
Cairo
Karachi
Lahore
Mumbai
Dhaka
Beijing
Tianjin
Seoul
Tokyo
Shanghai
Shenzhen
Guangzhou
92% JAPAN
32% INDIA
43% EGYPT
100% SINGAPORE
52% INDONESIA
24% TONGA
89% AUSTRALIA
SUB-SAHARAN AFRICA
71.8% of city dwellers live in slums.
30–50% lack access to safe water.
Child mortality is 2.5 times greater in slums than in rest of city.
Currently, 1 billion people live in slums.
This will double in the next 30 years to 2 billion.

Types of GOVERNMENT

People living in different countries have more or less say in how they are governed. In democracies, people can vote for their leaders, while in absolute monarchies or one-party states, people cannot choose who governs them.

THE WORLD'S GOVERNMENTS

This map shows the different types of government used by countries around the world.

USA

Cuba

UK

Spain

Cameroon

Switzerland
This Alpine country has a federal system made up of 26 regions called Cantons. It has no full-time president and presidential duties are carried out by one of the government's department heads.

TYPES OF GOVERNMENT

- **Republics • Eg: USA, India**
- **Constitutional monarchies • Eg: UK, Spain**
- **Absolute monarchies • Eg: UAE, Brunei**
- **Single political party or coalition • Eg: China, North Korea**
- **Other government systems • Switzerland**

Ruling parties
Republics make up nearly 75 per cent of the types of government around the world.

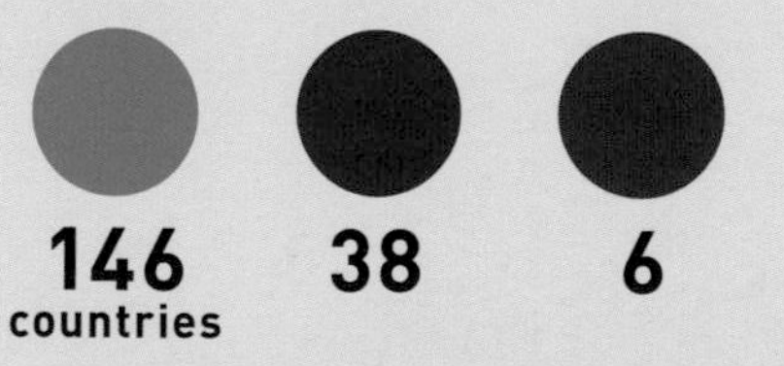

146 countries **38** **6** **7** **1**

Longest RULE

Paul Biya of Cameroon holds the record for the longest ruling non-royal national leader. He came to power on 30 June 1975 and in his time as president he has seen seven US presidents come and go.

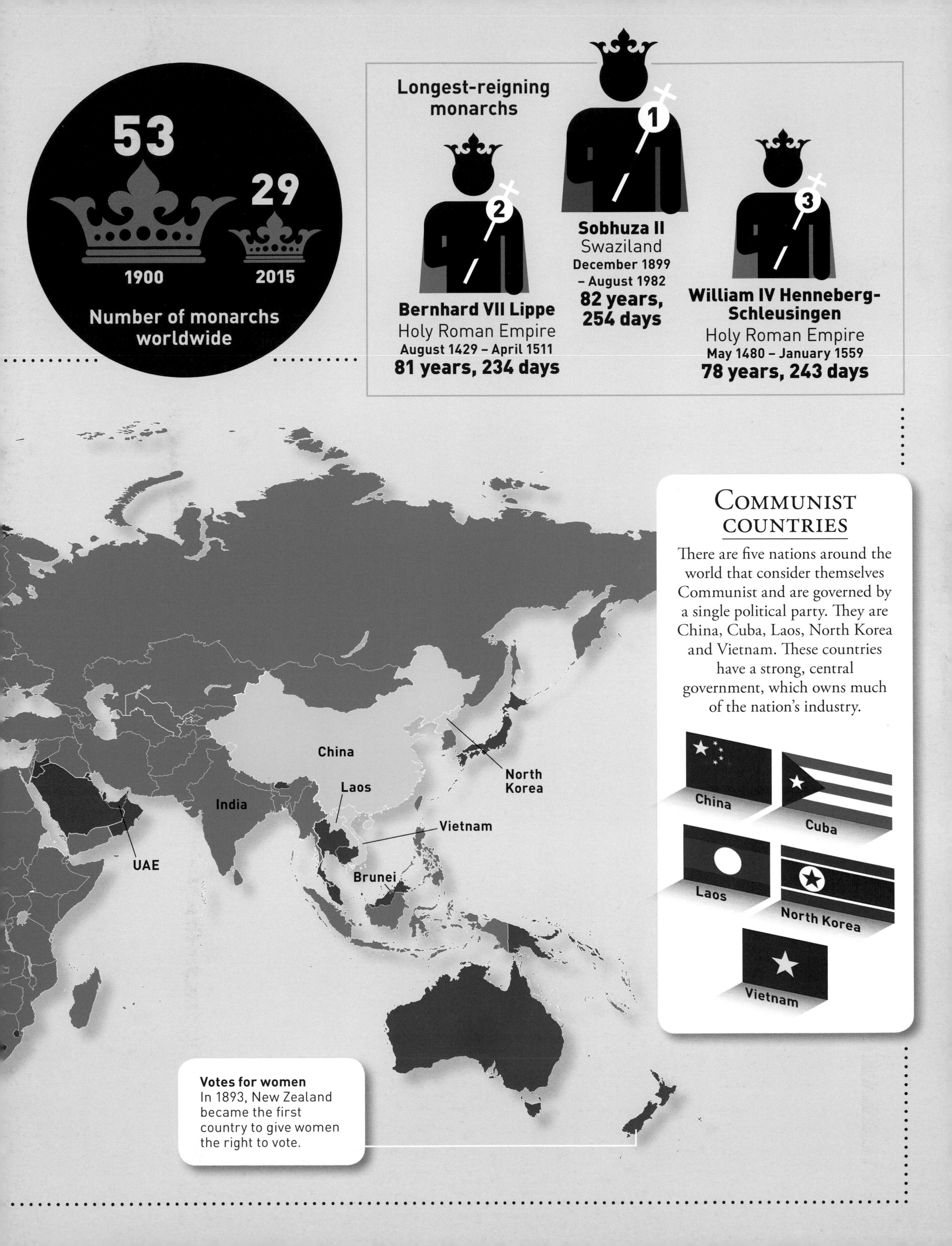
53
29
1900
2015
Number of monarchs worldwide
Longest-reigning monarchs
1
Sobhuza II
Swaziland
December 1899 – August 1982
82 years, 254 days
2
Bernhard VII Lippe
Holy Roman Empire
August 1429 – April 1511
81 years, 234 days
3
William IV Henneberg-Schleusingen
Holy Roman Empire
May 1480 – January 1559
78 years, 243 days
Communist countries
There are five nations around the world that consider themselves Communist and are governed by a single political party. They are China, Cuba, Laos, North Korea and Vietnam. These countries have a strong, central government, which owns much of the nation's industry.
China
Cuba
Laos
North Korea
Vietnam
China
Laos
North Korea
India
Vietnam
UAE
Brunei
Votes for women
In 1893, New Zealand became the first country to give women the right to vote.

Armed FORCES

The size of a country's armed forces depends on how involved it is in conflicts around the world and its relations with its neighbours. South Korea may be small, but tension with North Korea means that it maintains a large army.

GLOBAL ARMED FORCES

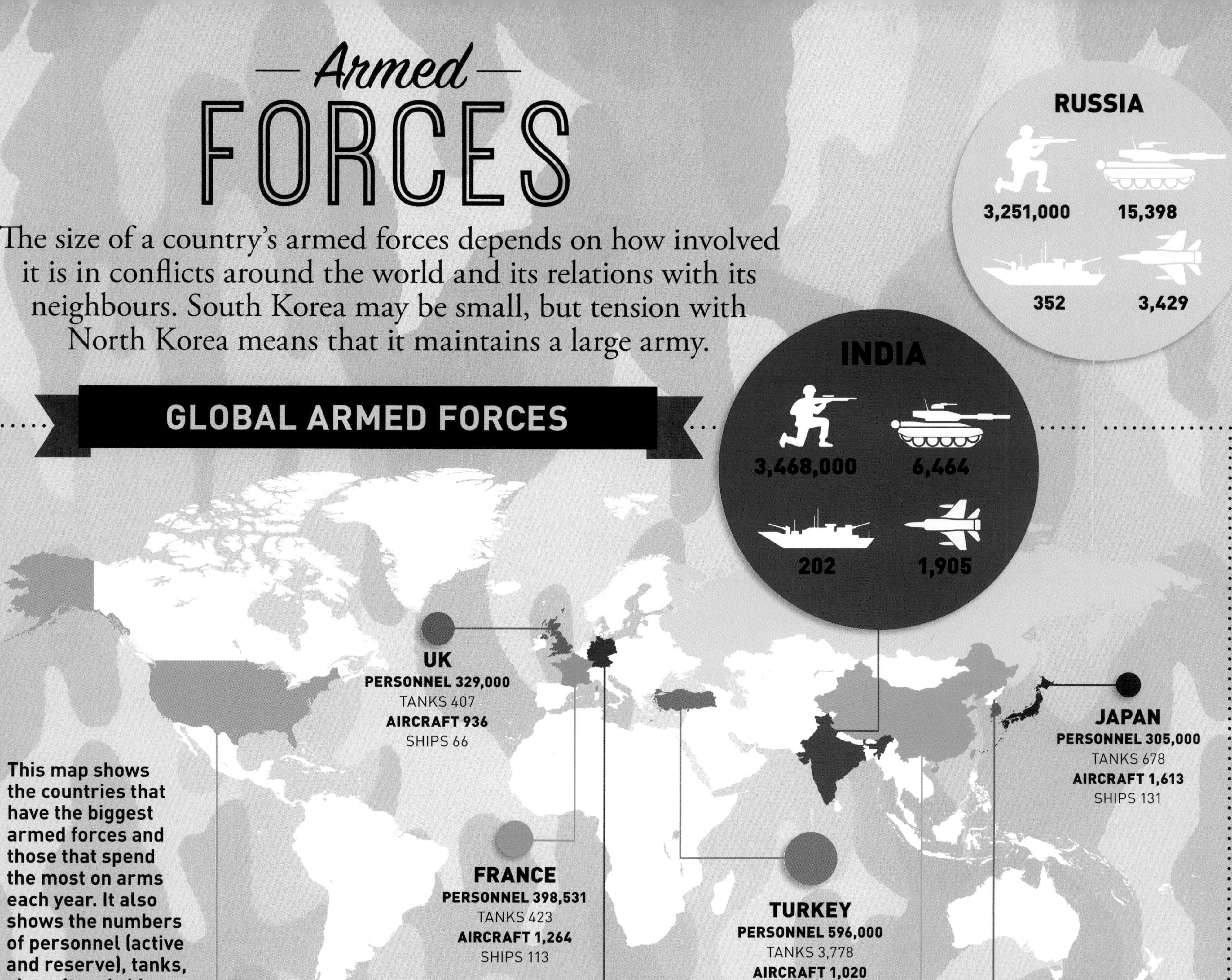

This map shows the countries that have the biggest armed forces and those that spend the most on arms each year. It also shows the numbers of personnel (active and reserve), tanks, aircraft and ships.

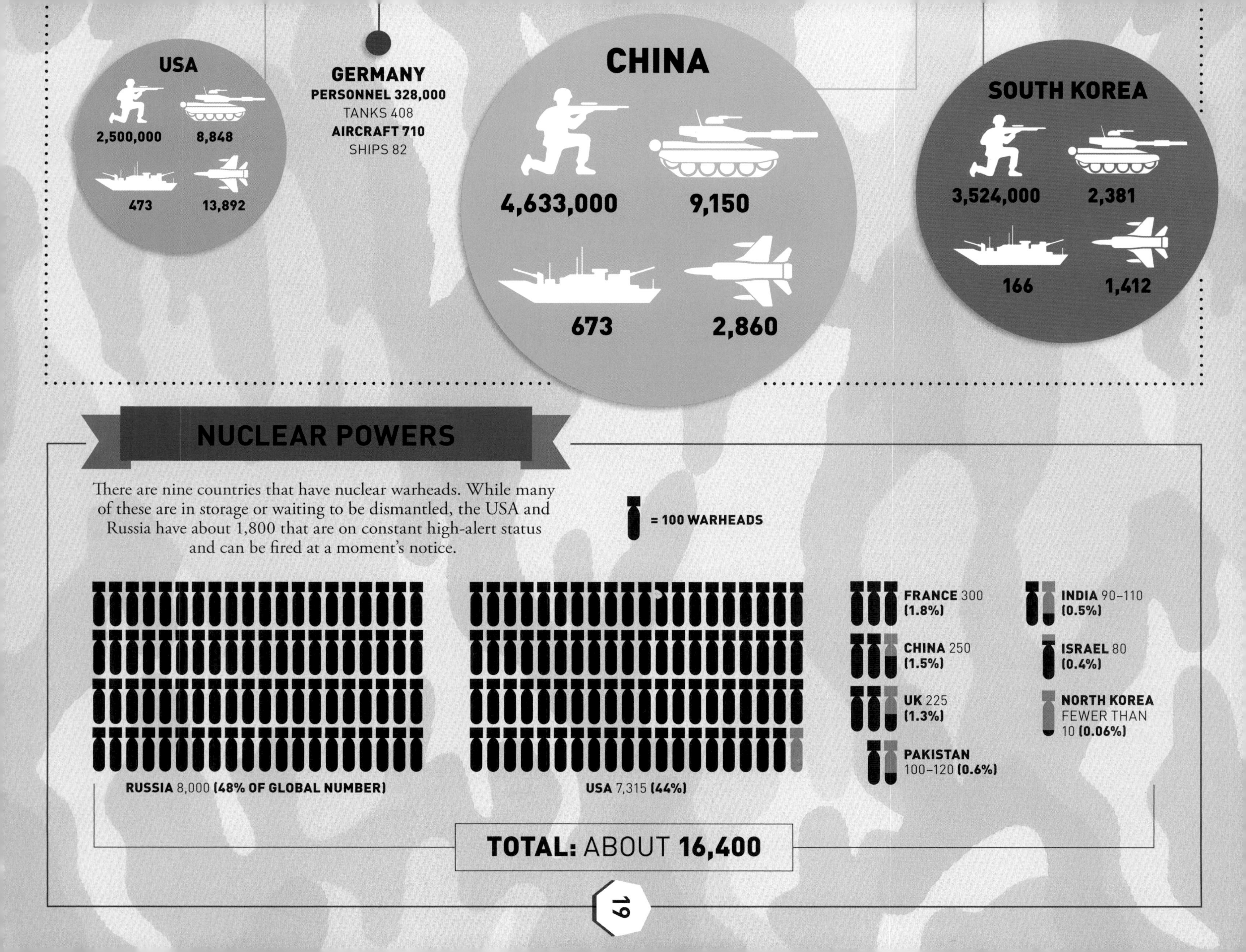
USA
2,500,000
8,848
473
13,892
GERMANY
PERSONNEL 328,000
TANKS 408
AIRCRAFT 710
SHIPS 82
CHINA
4,633,000
9,150
673
2,860
SOUTH KOREA
3,524,000
2,381
166
1,412
NUCLEAR POWERS
There are nine countries that have nuclear warheads. While many of these are in storage or waiting to be dismantled, the USA and Russia have about 1,800 that are on constant high-alert status and can be fired at a moment's notice.
= 100 WARHEADS
RUSSIA 8,000 (48% OF GLOBAL NUMBER)
USA 7,315 (44%)
FRANCE 300 (1.8%)
CHINA 250 (1.5%)
UK 225 (1.3%)
PAKISTAN 100–120 (0.6%)
INDIA 90–110 (0.5%)
ISRAEL 80 (0.4%)
NORTH KOREA FEWER THAN 10 (0.06%)
TOTAL: ABOUT 16,400

Getting HEAVY

Obesity is a problem in many parts of the world, with more than one-third of the people in some countries being extremely overweight. This is the result of eating too much and eating foods that are high in calories.

LEVELS OF OBESITY

This map shows the percentages of household income spent on food in different countries around the world and the levels of obesity. In general, wealthier countries spend a smaller percentage on food, but have higher levels of obesity.

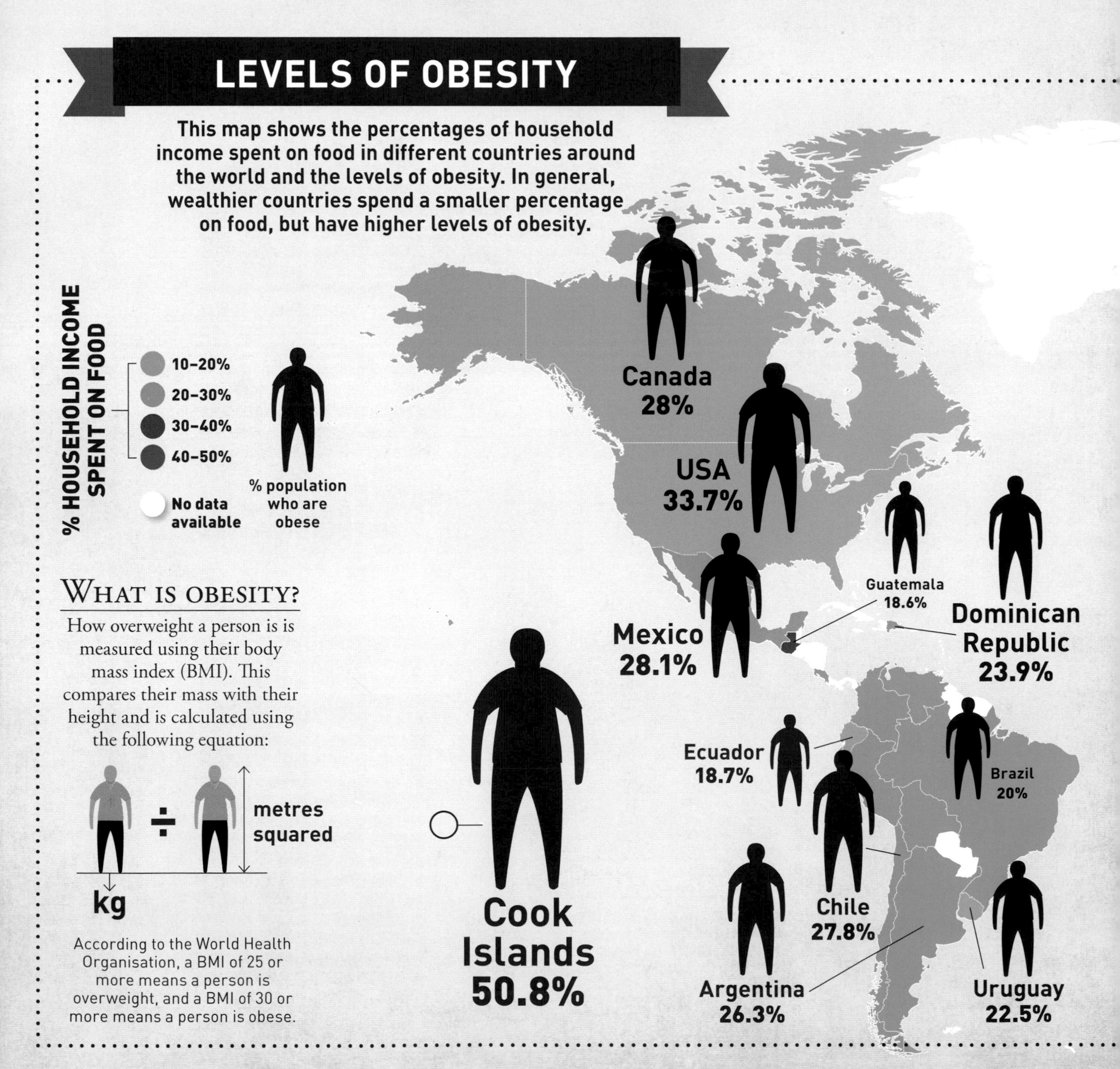

WHAT IS OBESITY?

How overweight a person is is measured using their body mass index (BMI). This compares their mass with their height and is calculated using the following equation:

According to the World Health Organisation, a BMI of 25 or more means a person is overweight, and a BMI of 30 or more means a person is obese.

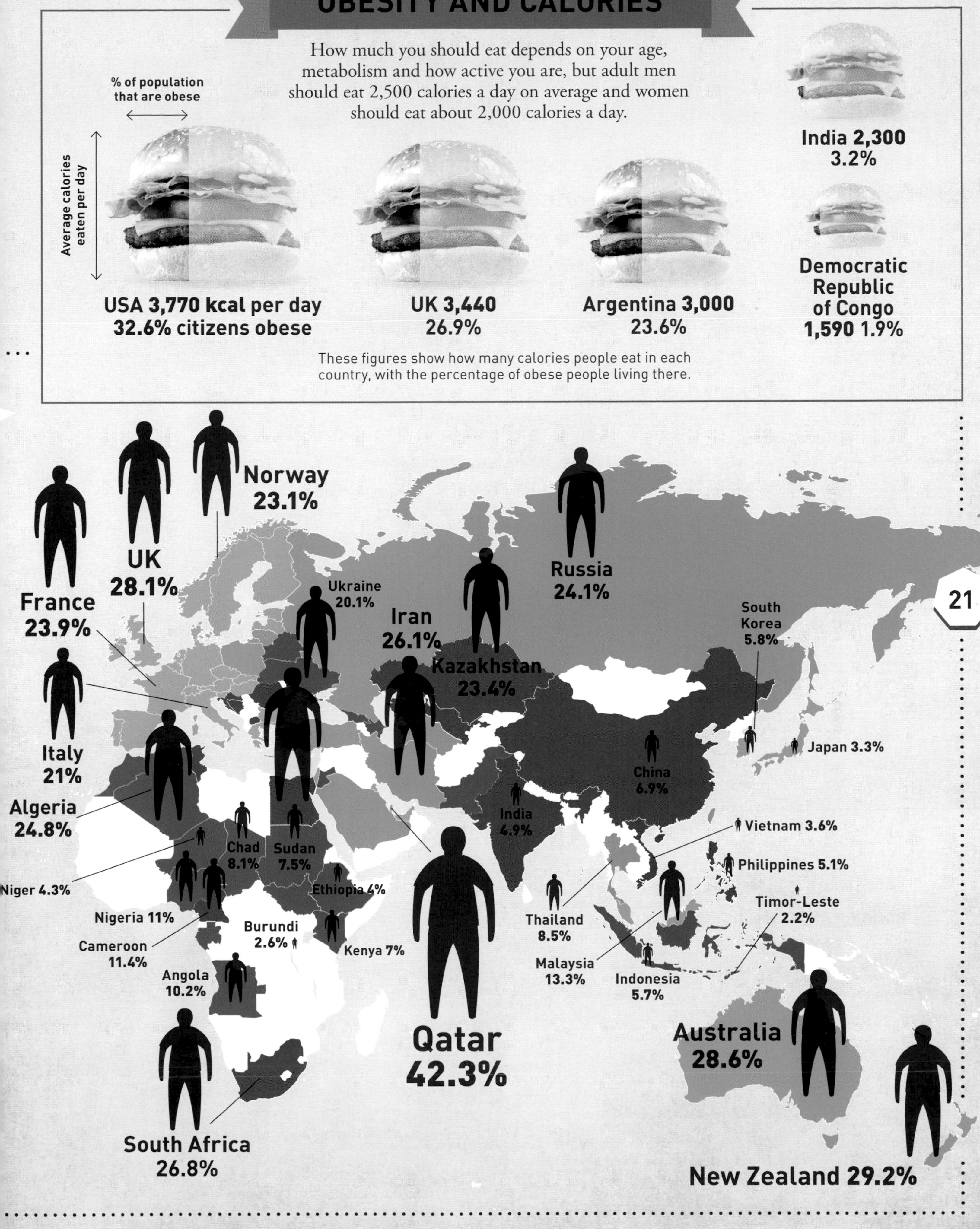

OBESITY AND CALORIES
How much you should eat depends on your age, metabolism and how active you are, but adult men should eat 2,500 calories a day on average and women should eat about 2,000 calories a day.
% of population that are obese
Average calories eaten per day
USA 3,770 kcal per day 32.6% citizens obese
UK 3,440 26.9%
Argentina 3,000 23.6%
India 2,300 3.2%
Democratic Republic of Congo 1,590 1.9%
These figures show how many calories people eat in each country, with the percentage of obese people living there.
Norway 23.1%
UK 28.1%
France 23.9%
Italy 21%
Algeria 24.8%
Ukraine 20.1%
Iran 26.1%
Kazakhstan 23.4%
Russia 24.1%
South Korea 5.8%
Japan 3.3%
China 6.9%
India 4.9%
Vietnam 3.6%
Philippines 5.1%
Timor-Leste 2.2%
Thailand 8.5%
Malaysia 13.3%
Indonesia 5.7%
Niger 4.3%
Chad 8.1%
Sudan 7.5%
Ethiopia 4%
Nigeria 11%
Cameroon 11.4%
Burundi 2.6%
Kenya 7%
Angola 10.2%
Qatar 42.3%
South Africa 26.8%
Australia 28.6%
New Zealand 29.2%
21

—Global—

LANGUAGES

There are more than 7,000 languages spoken around the world. Some of the most popular, such as Mandarin and Hindi, are spoken in countries with huge populations, while others, including English and Spanish, are widely spoken because of the colonial history of their original countries.

MAJOR LANGUAGES

This map shows what the major language is in each country in the world.

LANGUAGE

- **Arabic**
- **Bengali**
- **English**
- **German**
- **French**
- **Hindi**
- **Mandarin Chinese**
- **Portuguese**
- **Russian**
- **Spanish**
- **Other, such as Italian and Greek**

WRITING SYSTEMS

Written languages use a system of symbols to represent various letters, groups of letters, sounds or even entire words. These symbols range from simple lines and shapes to complex illustrations.

Latin alphabet

Latin (used in many European languages)

Ελληνικο αλφαβητο

Greek (used in Greek)

LANGUAGES OF THE INTERNET

The large number of internet users in North America, the UK and Australasia means that English is by far the most common language used to search the internet.

Languages of Internet users (millions of users)

MOST POPULAR LANGUAGES

At one point in its history, the British Empire covered almost one-third of the globe. This is why today English is spoken in more countries than any other language. Other former empires include Portugal, France and Spain, and their languages are spoken around the world, while Arabic dominates nations in northern Africa and the Middle East.

Portuguese 11

French 51

Arabic 59

English 101 countries

Russian 11

Spanish 31

Кириллица
алфавит

Cyrillic (used in Russian)

Kanji (used in Japanese)

Holiday TIME

Key factors that affect how much time people spend on holiday and where they go include cost, the amount of holidays they can have and what their own country has to offer in terms of facilities and climate.

MOST POPULAR DESTINATIONS

These figures show how many foreign tourists visit each of these countries every year and the most popular tourist attractions.

1 **FRANCE** 84,726,000

Most visited attraction
Notre Dame Cathedral, Paris

2 **USA** 69,768,000

Most visited attraction
Times Square, New York City

3 **SPAIN** 60,661,000

Most visited attraction
Alhambra Palace, Granada

5 **ITALY** 47,704,000

Most visited attraction
St. Peter's Basilica, Vatican City

TAKING TIME OFF

These figures show the countries that guarantee their workers the highest and lowest amount of paid holiday.

Countries with the most time off (days)

10 JAPAN
5 CHINA
0 USA

Countries with the least time off (days)

4 CHINA 55,686,000

Most visited attraction **Forbidden City, Beijing**

Tourist money

Tourists and holiday makers can bring a lot of money into a country. These figures show which countries earn the most from tourism.

Earnings from tourism
(US$ billions per year)

ITALY US$41.2

CHINA US$50

FRANCE US$53.6

SPAIN US$55.9

USA US$126.2

Education AND LITERACY

The ability to read and write is the basis of a good education, but levels and abilities vary greatly around the world, depending largely on the wealth of the country. Levels of literacy and education can also vary between men and women, even in the same country.

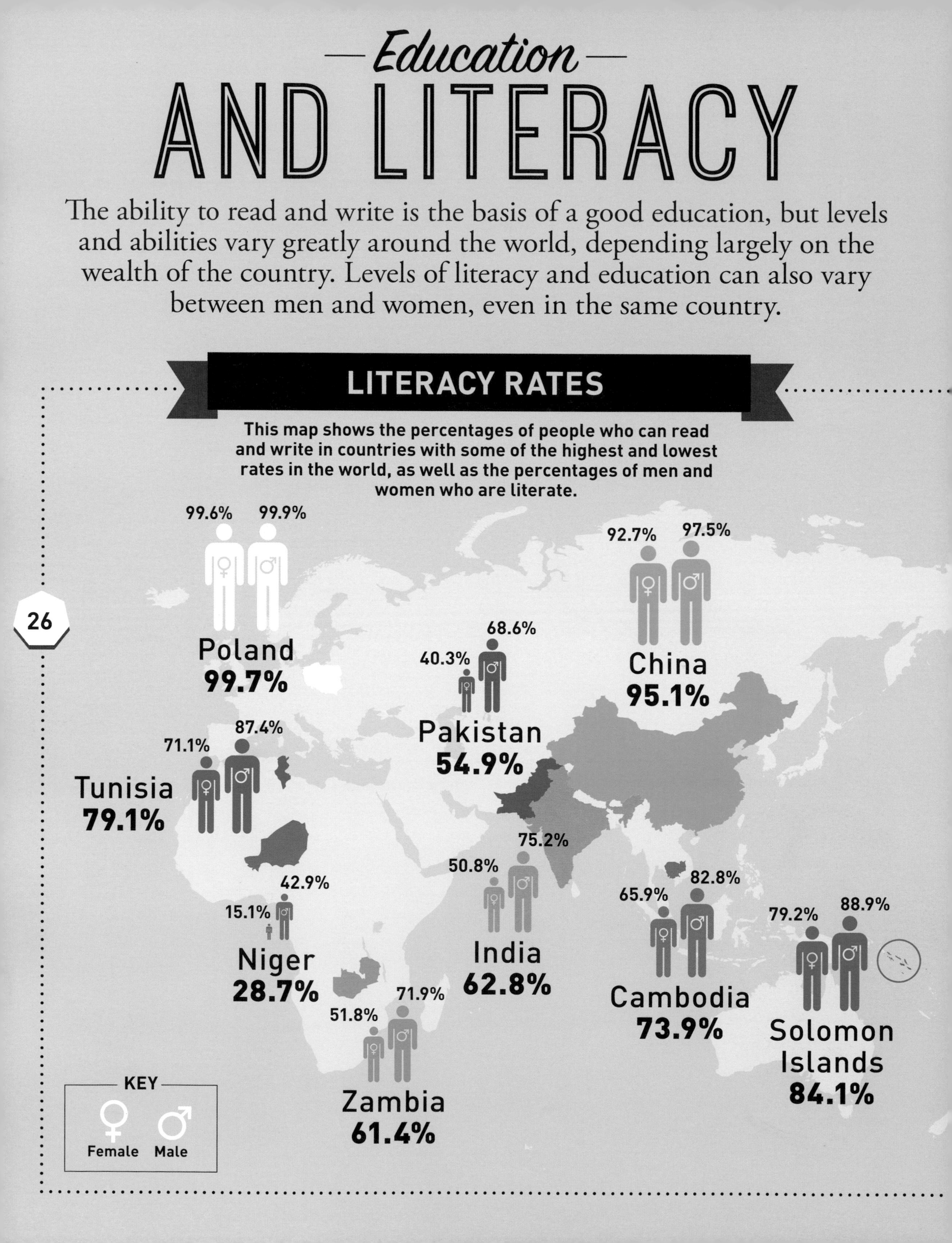

YEARS SPENT IN EDUCATION

Wealthier countries, such as Australia, usually spend more on their schools, universities and colleges than poorer countries, such as the African country of Niger. As such, people in wealthier countries will spend longer in school, gaining a higher literacy rate and more qualifications.

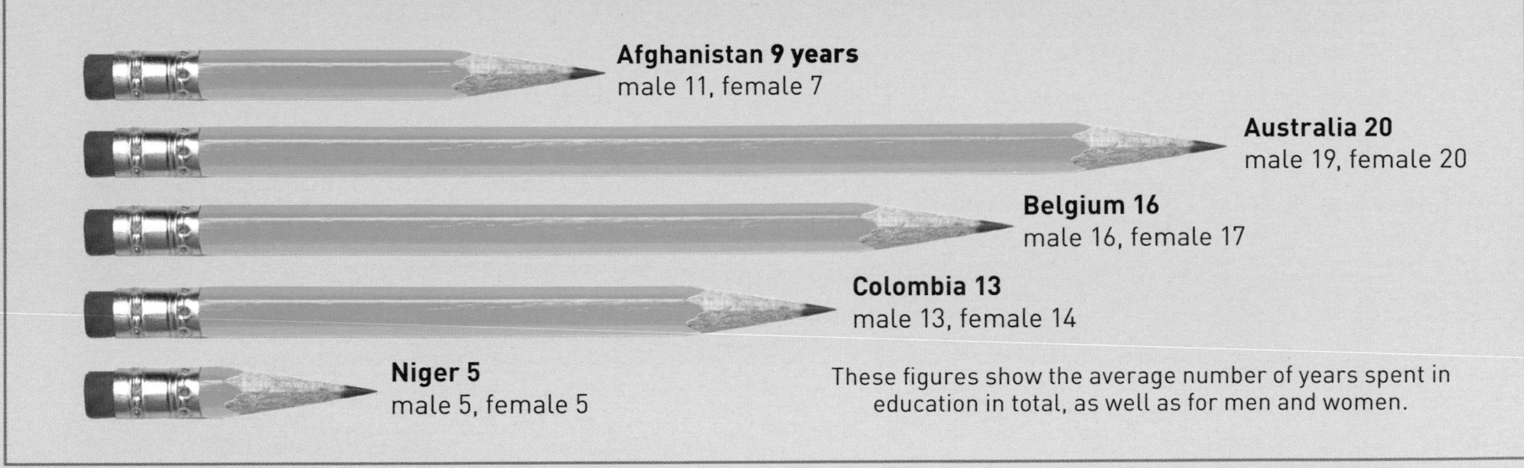

These figures show the average number of years spent in education in total, as well as for men and women.

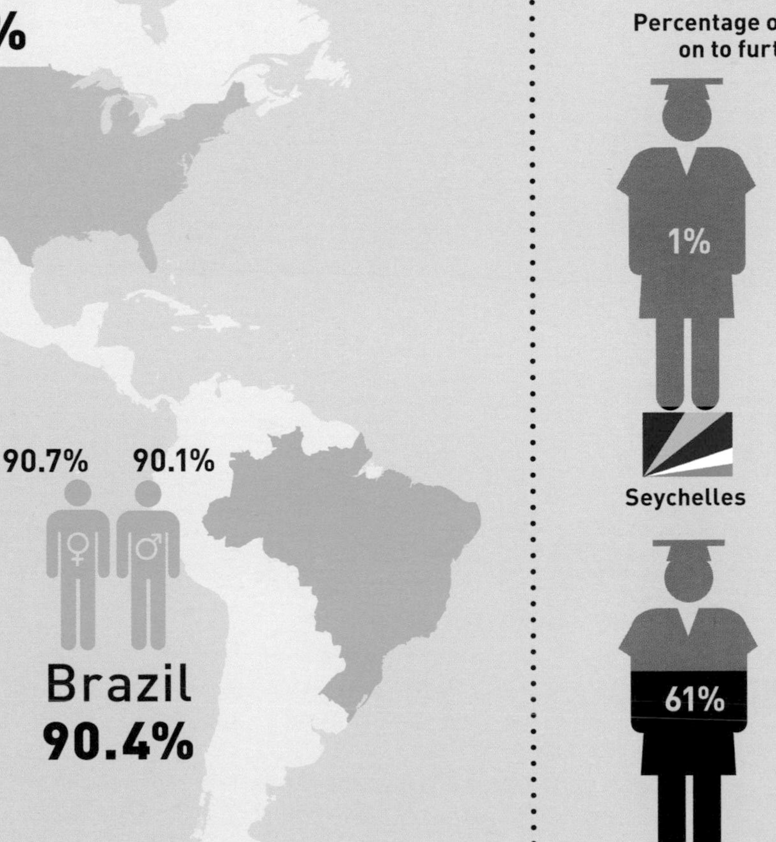

Female 79.7%

Male 88.6%

84.1%

WORLD AVERAGE LITERACY

BEYOND SCHOOL

Going on to further education at a college or university allows a person to study for a degree or other similar qualification. People living in wealthier countries are more likely to go to college or university.

Percentage of population going on to further education

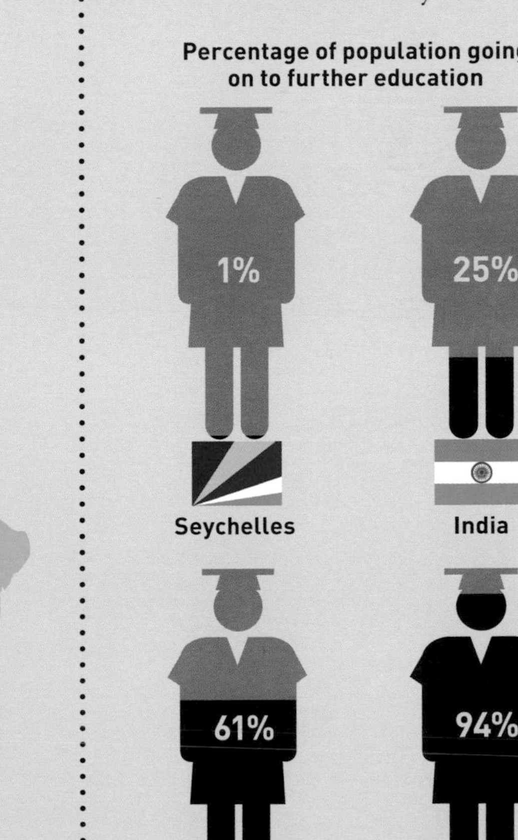

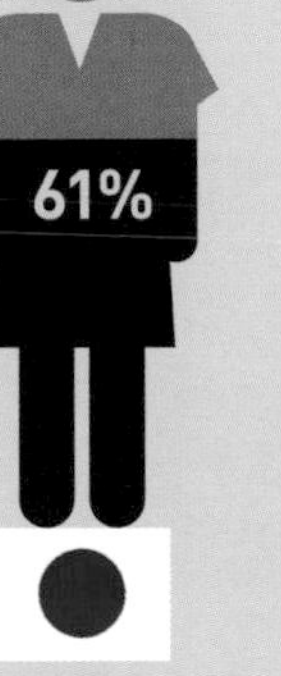

RELIGION

More than 80 per cent of the world's population, or 5.8 billion people, are members of a religion. Of these 5.8 billion, 2.2 billion are Christian, 1.6 billion are Muslim, 1 billion are Hindu, 500 million are Buddhist and 14 million are Jewish.

MAJOR RELIGIONS

This map shows which religion is worshipped by the majority of people in each country around the world.

USA

Christian **78.5%**
Jewish **1.6%**
Buddhist **0.7%**
Muslim **0.6%**
won't say **4%**
non-religious **12.1%**
other or unspecified **2.5%**

USA

THE VATICAN
The Vatican is the centre of the Christian Roman Catholic religion. Located in the centre of Rome, Italy, it is the home of the Pope, who is the head of the Catholic church.

NIGERIA

NIGERIA

Christian **40%**
Muslim **50%**
other or unspecified **10%**

Sacred sites

Scattered around the world are several places that are very important to the major religions. These sacred sites hold important buildings or venues where millions of people travel to on special journeys called pilgrimages.

RELIGION

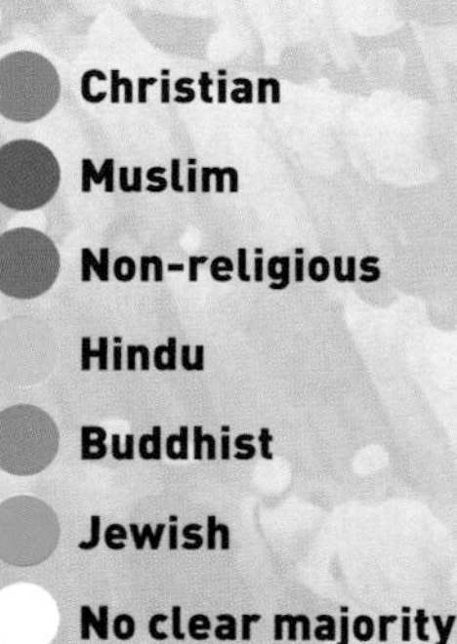

JERUSALEM, ISRAEL/WEST BANK
The city of Jerusalem is a sacred site for three major religions: Judaism, Christianity and Islam.

MECCA, SAUDI ARABIA
Every year, millions of Muslims make a pilgrimage, or Hajj, to Mecca, Saudi Arabia. Mecca is the birthplace of the prophet Muhammad and the holiest city in the religion of Islam.

AMRITSAR, INDIA
The Golden Temple, or Harmandir Sahib, at Amritsar in India is the centre of the Sikh religion.

VARANASI, INDIA
Located on the banks of the Ganges river, Varanasi is one of the most sacred sites in Hinduism. Millions of people come to the city to bathe in the river's holy waters.

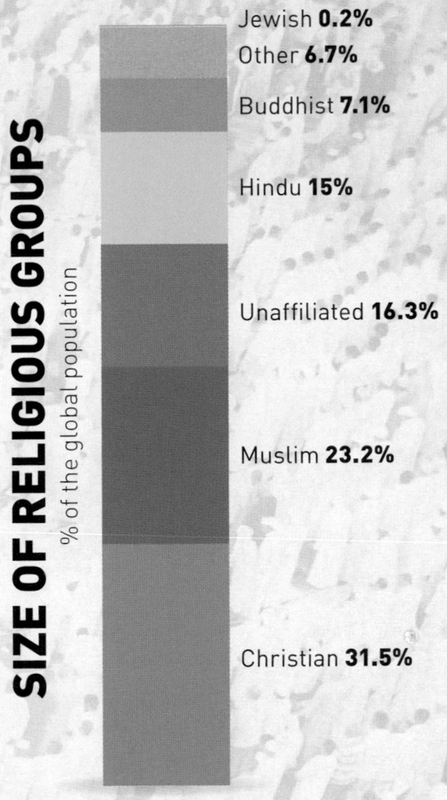

SIZE OF RELIGIOUS GROUPS

% of the global population

Jewish **0.2%**
Other **6.7%**
Buddhist **7.1%**
Hindu **15%**
Unaffiliated **16.3%**
Muslim **23.2%**
Christian **31.5%**

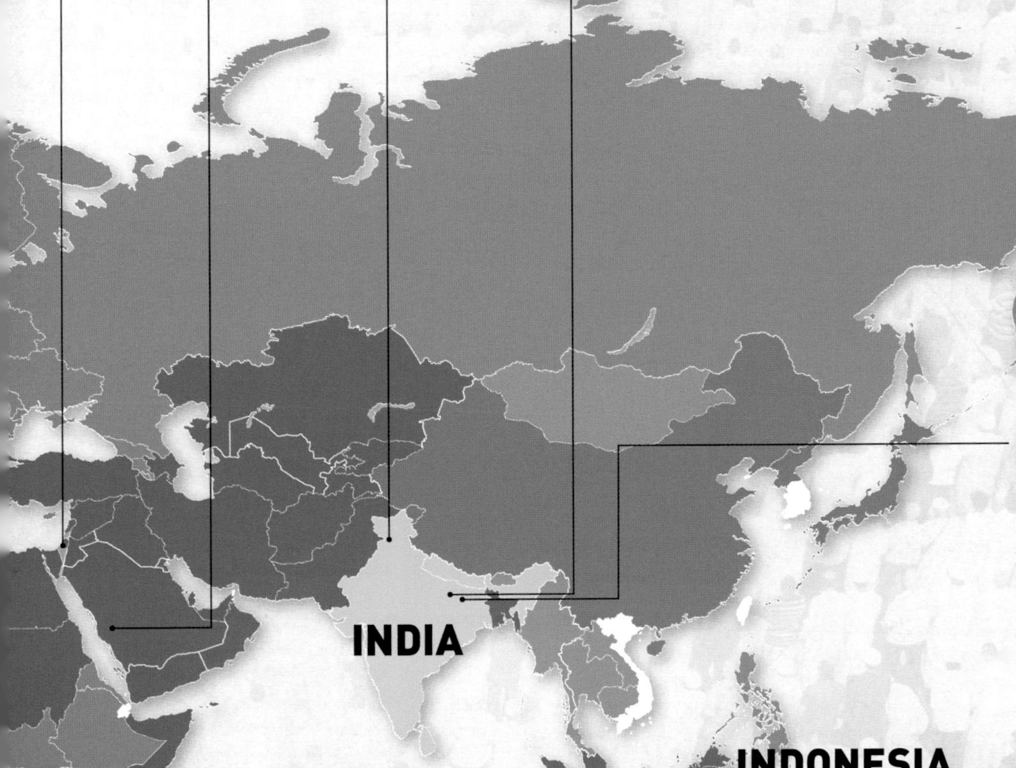

BODH GAYA, INDIA
Said to be the spot where Gautama Buddha achieved enlightenment, Bodh Gaya is a sacred pilgrimage site to members of the Buddhist religion.

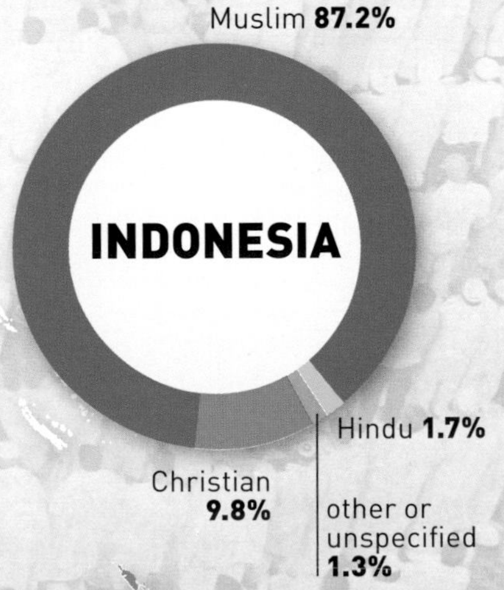

INDIA

INDONESIA

INDIA

Hindu **80.5%**
Muslim **13.4%**
Christian **2.3%**
Sikh **1.9%**
other or unspecified **1.9%**

INDONESIA

Muslim **87.2%**
Christian **9.8%**
Hindu **1.7%**
other or unspecified **1.3%**

Mapping the WORLD

The maps in this book are two-dimensional representations of our ball-shaped world. Maps allow us to display a huge range of information, including the size of the countries and where people live.

Projections

Converting the three-dimensional world into a two-dimensional map can produce different views, called projections. These projections can show different areas of the Earth.

GLOBE
Earth is shaped like a ball, with the landmasses wrapped around it.

CURVED
Some maps show parts of the world as they would appear on this ball.

FLAT
Maps of the whole world show the landmasses laid out flat. The maps in this book use projections like this.

Types of map

Different types of map can show different types of information. Physical maps show physical features, such as mountains and rivers, while political maps show countries and cities. Schematic maps show specific types of information, such as routes on an underground train network, and they may not necessarily show things in excatly the right place.

Physical map

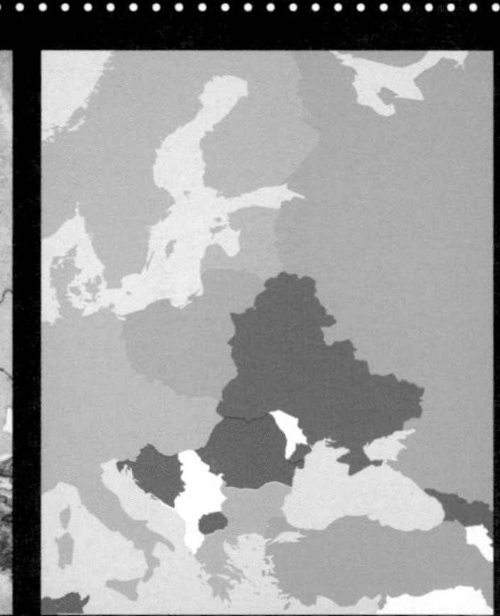

Political map

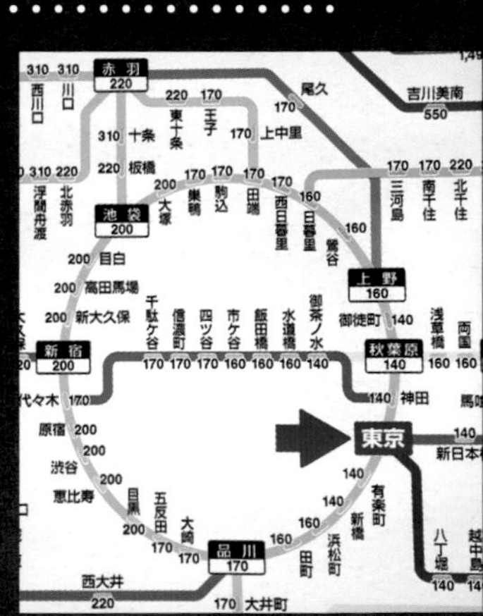

Schematic map

Map symbols

Maps use lots of symbols to show information, such as blue lines for rivers and dots for cities. Some of the symbols in this book show the locations of subjects, or the symbols are different sizes to represent different values – the bigger the symbol, the greater the value.

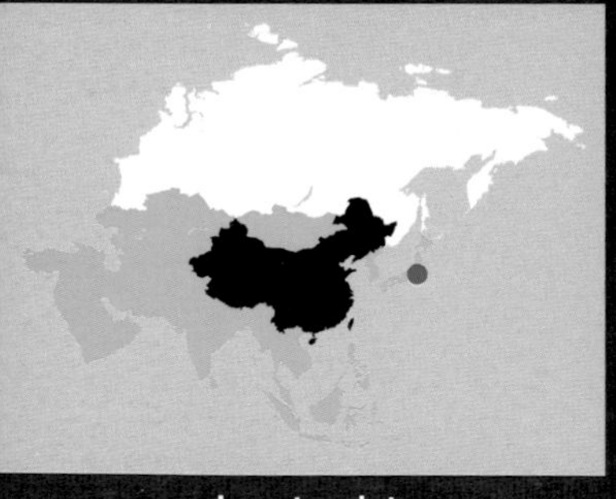

Locator dot

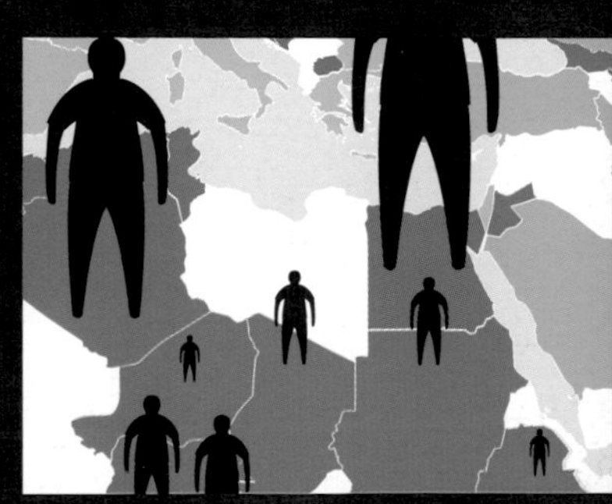

Scaled symbols

GLOSSARY

ANCESTOR
An individual or a species from which a modern person or species has descended.

FAVELA
The Portuguese name given to the enormous shanty towns that grow up in and around major cities throughout Brazil.

FERTILITY RATE
The average number of children that a woman will give birth to in her lifetime.

GROSS DOMESTIC PRODUCT (GDP)
The value of the goods and services that are produced by a country over a year. The GDP can be shown as the total value produced by an entire country over a year or as the average for each person living in that country (per capita).

HEALTHCARE
The facilities on offer in a country that look after and protect a person's health. They include clinics, hospitals, nurses and doctors.

LAND BRIDGE
A strip of land linking two large landmasses. During the last ice age, land bridges appeared linking America to Asia and Australia to Asia. These allowed prehistoric humans and animals to migrate to these continents.

LIFE EXPECTANCY
The number of years a person can expect to live for. Life expectancy depends on a number of factors, including where a person lives, whether they are male or female, how long their parents lived for and their lifestyle.

LITERACY
A person's ability to read and write.

MIGRATION
The movement of animals and humans from one region to another usually in search of food, water or a place to raise young and live.

MONARCHY
A type of government where the head of state is a king or queen.

OBESITY
A medical condition where a person has accumulated so much fat that it threatens his or her health.

PILGRIMAGE
A journey made to a holy place.

REPUBLIC
A type of government where the population votes in the people who will govern them.

RESPIRATORY
Relating to your breathing system, including the lungs and airways.

SANITATION
The safe disposal of waste, including human waste, and stopping people from coming into contact with that waste.

URBANISATION
The rate at which people move from the countryside and into towns and cities.

WARHEAD
The explosive part of a bomb or missile. Warheads can be conventional or nuclear.

WEBSITES

WWW.NATIONALGEOGRAPHIC.COM/KIDS-WORLD-ATLAS/MAPS.HTML
The map section of the National Geographic website where readers can create their own maps and study maps covering different topics.

WWW.MAPSOFWORLD.COM/KIDS/
Website with a comprehensive collection of maps covering a wide range of themes that are aimed at students and available to download and print out.

HTTPS://WWW.CIA.GOV/LIBRARY/PUBLICATIONS/THE-WORLD-FACTBOOK/
The information resource for the Central Intelligence Agency (CIA), this offers detailed facts and figures on a range of topics, such as population and transport, about every single country in the world.

WWW.KIDS-WORLD-TRAVEL-GUIDE.COM
Website with facts and travel tips about a host of countries from around the world.

INDEX

The publisher would like to thank the following for their kind permission to reproduce their photographs:

Key: (t) top; (c) centre; (b) bottom; (l) left; (r) right

Cover, 1br 24-25 and 25t istockphoto.com/rypson, 3a and 30cl NASA, 6-7 istockphoto.com/DRB Images, LLC, 11br istockphoto.com/Carlos_bcn, 12-13 istockphoto.com/spanteldotru, 14-15 istockphoto.com/tomlamela, 18-19 istockphoto.com/ozgurartug, 21t all istockphoto.com/drewhadley, 23t istockphoto.com/Courtney Keating, 24cr istockphoto.com/W6, 24 cl istockphoto.com/dibrova, 24bl istockphoto.com/WillSelarep, 24br istockphoto.com/Nikada, 25bl istockphoto.com/06photo, 27t all istockphoto.com/bluestocking, 28-29 istockphoto.com/Zurijeta, 28cr istockphoto.com/Nikada, 29t istockphoto.com/Yoav Peled, 29tl istockphoto.com/afby71, 29tc istockphoto.com/traveler1116, 29m istockphoto.com/oytun karadayi, 29cr istockphoto.com/Rufous52, 30c istockphoto.com/nicoolay, 30cr istockphoto.com/Manakin

Every attempt has been made to clear copyright. Should there be any inadvertent omission, please apply to the publisher for rectification.

The website addresses (URLs) included in this book were valid at the time of going to press. However, it is possible that contents or addresses may have changed since the publication of this book. No responsibility for any such changes can be accepted by either the author or the Publisher.

GET THE PICTURE

Welcome to the world of visual learning! Icons, pictograms and infographics present information in a new and appealing way.